A Compendious Dictionary of the English Language

NOAH WEBSTER

1806

TABLE OF CONTENTS

FORWARD

DISTRICT of CONNECTICUT,
BE it remembered, That on the fifteenth day of January in the thirtieth year
of the Independence of the United States of America, NOAH WEBSTER,
Esq. of the said District, hath deposited in this office the title of a book the
right whereof he claims as Author, in the words following, to wit,—" A
Compendious Dictionary of the English Language. In which five thousand
words are added to the number found in the best English Compends; The
Orthography is in some instances corrected; The Pronunciation marked by
an accent, or other suitable direction; And the Definitions of many words
amended and improved To which are added for the benefit of the
merchant, the student and the traveller,—I. Tables of the moneys of most
of the commercial nations in the world, with the value expressed in sterling
and cents.—2. Tables of weights and measures, ancient and modern, with
the proportion between the several weights used in the principal cities of
Europe.—3. The Divisions of time among the Jews, Greeks and Romans,
with a table exhibiting the Roman manner of dating.—4. An official List of
the Post-Offices in the United States, with the states and counties in which
they are respectively situated, and the distance of each from the seat of
government.—5. The number of inhabitants in the United States, with the
amount of exports.—6. New and interesting Chronological Tables of
remarkable events and discoveries. —By Noah Webster, Esq."
In conformity to the acts of the Congress of the United States entitled "An
act for the encouragement of learning, by securing the copies of maps,
charts and books, to authors and proprietors of such copies, during the
times therein mentioned."

SIMEON BALDWIN, Clerk of the District of Connecticut.
A true copy of record. Examined and sealed by S. BALDWIN, Clk Dist.
Cont.

PREFACE

ON the first publication of my Institutes of the English Language, more than twenty years ago, that eminent classical scholar and divine, the late Dr. Goodrich of Durham, recommended to me to complete a system of elementary principles for the instruction of youth in the English language, by compiling and publishing a dictionary. Whatever respect I was inclined to pay to that gentleman's opinion, I could not, at that time, believe myself qualified for such an undertaking; and various private considerations afterwards interposed to retard its execution. My studies however have occasionally had reference to an ultimate accomplishment of such a work; and for a few years past, they have been directed immediately to that object. As I have advanced in my investigations, I have been, at every step, more and more impressed with the importance of this work; and an acquaintance with the Saxon language, the mother tongue of the English, has convinced me, that a careful revision of our present dictionaries is absolutely necessary to a correct knowledge of the language.

To men who have been accustomed to repose almost implicit confidence in the authors of our principal dictionaries and grammars, it may appear at first incredible, that such writers as Johnson and Lowth, should have mistaken many of the fundamental principles of the language. But that such is the fact, will appear certain to any man who will read a few pages in a Saxon author. For example, those distinguished scholars, following the opinion of Wallis, suppose own, to be a participle of the verb to owe; when a moderate acquaintance with the Saxon will show that it has not the remotest connection with that verb. Indeed a man, well versed in etymology, will at once see that the improbability, not to say, impossibility, that two words of such distinct significations, as to be indebted and to possess, can have sprung from a common root. Own, in Saxon agen, agenen, agenne, is derived from the verb agan, to possess; the g being in

Saxon a mere guttural aspirate, suppressed in the progress of civilization, as in nagel, nail, flagen, finy, agen, own. "Each, says Johnson, denotes, 1st. Either of two. 2d. Every one of any number. This sense is rare except in poetry." To prove the last remark to be an error, we need not resort to the Saxon, for every book we read, and every conversation we hear, demonstrates the fact. "The princes of Israel, being twelve men, each one was for the house of his fathers."—Numb. 1. 44. This is the true original import of the word; it has no appropriate reference to two, more than to ten thousand. "Thyder man ne mihte geseglian on anum monthe, gyf man on nyht wicode and ælce dæge hæfde amberne wind." "Thither a man could not sail in a month, if he should watch at night and each day should have a fair wind." Alfred's Orosius, Ch. 1. See also page 61, 63, 79, 219. Lond. 1773. and Sax. Ch. by Gibson, page 185, 186. The second definition of Johnson is therefore the only true one; but not well expressed.

"'Either, says Lowth, is often used improperly for each; each signifies both taken separately; either properly signifies only the one or the other, taken disjunctively." In pursuance of this false rule, he condemns such passages as this. "They crucified two others with him, on either side one and Jesus in the midst." But the sense in which the word is here used in the true primitive one, and still used by the best writers. "Mycell wæl thær on ægthere hand gefeoll." "There was great slaughter on either hand." Sax. Ch. 134. "Thet ægther hiora on other hawede." "That either of them might see the other," p. 133. "Swithe mycel here ægther ge land-here ge scip-here of Swatheode." "A very great army, either land army, and ship-army from Sweden." That is both. p. 153. So far is Lowth's rule from the truth, that either, in our primitive writers, was rarely or never used in a disjunctive sense. In reading considerable volumes of the best Saxon writings, I have not found a single instance. Its disjunctive use is modern; but its original sense is still in use and perfectly proper.

"There full in view, to either host displayed." Hoole's Tasso, 22, 602

The passages in scripture, the language of which Lowth condemns, are precisely correct.

Says Lowth, "the prepositions to and for are often understood, chiefly before the pronoun, as give me the book; get me some paper, "that is, to me, for me." But in truth these expressions contain the true dative case of the Saxon; me is in the dative, like the latin mihi, and no preposition was ever used before the pronoun in these and the like phrases.

Says Lowth, "the preposition in or on is often understood before nouns expressing time; as this day, next month, last year; that is, on this day, andc." It is a little strange that so excellent a classical scholar as Dr. Lowth should have made this mistake. The Saxons, like the Greeks, used nouns of time without preceding prepositions. Thus they used, dæges, and nihtes, day and night, in the genitive, like the Greeks—and continuance of time was marked by the accusative, as in the latin language—thry dages, three days. This construction is of the highest antiquity; the Greek, Latin and Saxon languages all having a common origin, the idiom in question is to be considered as primitive; no preposition, in these cases, having been ever used and none being understood.

Lesser, says Johnson, is a barbarous corruption of less, formed by the vulgar from the habit of terminating comparatives in er. He denounces worser in the same style; and Lowth and all other grammarians repeat the sentence of proscription. Had these authors ever read a Saxon book with attention, they must have perceived their error. Lesser and worser are not double comparatives, but mere corruptions of lesse, læssa; wyrse, wyrsa, which were simple comparatives in the Saxon. Worser is now obsolete; but lesser maintains its ground as the equivalent of less. See Sax. Ch. p. 171. Alf. Oros, page 16, 17.

"He is mistaken, tho never so wise," Johnson thinks to be justly accused of solicism. But this is the true original Saxon idiom—"Nan man ne dorste slean otherne man, neesde he næfre swa mocel yfel gedon with thone otherne. "No man durst slay another, let him have done to him never so much evil." Sax. Ch. 190. The true resolution of the phrase is, let him have done so much evil to him as never before—or as never was done before — a very forcible manner of expressing the idea. "If I make my hands never so clean"—"Charm he never so wisely"—"Ask me never so much dowry and gift"—are legitimate English phrases, which our best writers have used; which are preserved in popular practice, and which the grammarian has no right to proscribe—How would the elegant Addison, that pre-eminent writer of unadulterated English, smile, were he to rise from the grave, and see this genuine idiom in the Spectator, stigmatized, by a hypercritical Editor, as bad grammar, and printed in Italics!

"The neuter pronoun it, says Murray, on the authority of Campbell, is sometimes omitted and understood—thus we say, "as appears" "as follows," for, "as it appears," "as it follows." This remark is a gross and mischievous error, arising from the author's not understanding the word as, which has most absurdly been classed with conjunctions. The truth is, as is a relative pronoun, equivalent to who, which or that; as may be seen in the German, the elder sister of the English. There is scarcely a page of any English book in which we do not observe it, both in the nominative and objective cases, representing either persons or things. In the phrases mentioned, as appears, as is the nominative to the verb—being only another word for which—which appears—which follows— and by inserting it, "which it follows," we convert the phrases into a palpable nonsense.

"That," says Lowth, "is used indifferently both of persons and things; but perhaps would be more properly confined to the latter." Campbell, in his

Philosophy of Rhetotic, remarks upon this observation of Lowth, that "there are cases wherein we cannot conveniently dispense with this relative as applied to persons:" as in this sentece, "Who that has any sense of religion would have argued thus?"

Murray remarks, that, "that as a relative, is often used to prevent the too frequent repetition of who and which," and in another place, copying from Campbell, that we cannot conveniently dispense with this relative as applied to persons."

The smallest acquaintance with our mother tongue, would show that these writers have inverted the true state of the fact, and that instead of usurping the province of who and which, that, is the primitive relative whose place is usurped by who and which.

In the Saxon, who was never a simple relative. In the volumes I have read, it does not occur in that character, in a single instance. It occurs very rarely, perhaps not ten times in an octavo volume, and then only as an interrogative, or in the sense of whoever, or any person, equivalent to the Latin quispiam or quisquis at the beginning of sentences. From the fragments of the Roman laws of the first kings and of the twelve tables which are still extant, there is reason to believe that this was the primitive sense of qui, or who. The Saxons used for a relative, the and that, which we have blended into one word, that. This is our true primitive relative; and any person who will examine the present translation of the bible, or the customary language of conversation, will find that it maintains its place as the principal relative in the language. It still holds a primary, and not a subordinate place.

These examples are sufficient to demonstrate the importance of investigating the original of the English Language; and how much mischief has been done by men who have compiled elementary books, without qualifying themselves by such previous investigation.

More formidable objections than these may be made to our present grammars; but the limits of this preface will not permit a full discussion of this subject which is reserved for another work. It is proper to confine my observations, in this place, to the more immediate objects of this publication.

Of the numerous dictionaries of the English Language which are used in the United States, Bailey's and Johnson's are those which are considered as containing the most original materials; and Johnson's in particular is the fund from which modern compilers have selected the substance of their works. On Bailey's orthography, etymologies and definition of mathematical terms, Johnson has made little improvement. The excellence of Johnson's work consits chiefly in presenting to the reader the various different significations of words distinctly arranged and exemplified. On this part of the work, the author has bestowed uncommon pains, and has usually displayed critical discernments aided by extensive and various reading. Yet even in this part of his dictionary, many errors escaped his pen, and some of them are so obvious that it is not easy to number them with the effects of ordinary negligence.

Thus according to Johnson's definition, an administratix is a woman "who administers in consequence of a will"; and obvious as the error is, we find it copied into Sheridan, Walker, Jones, andc.

Misnomer, says Johnson, is "an indictment or any other act vacated by a wrong name"; an incorrect definition, copied into Sheridan, Walker, Perry, Entick, Jones, Ash, andc.

Obligee Johnson defines to be "one bound by a legal and written contract"—the true definition of obligor; and this obvious blunder is transcribed into Sheridan, Walker, Entick, Perry, Ash and Jones.

Such mistakes are the more surprising, because the compiler had Jacob and Cowel before him, and usually copied the definition of law terms from one or the other of those authorities. These errors are corrected by Mason; but others have escaped his notice. For example, Johnson's definition of murder is not technically correct, as it would answer equally well for manslaughter; yet Mason has not noticed the inaccuracy. Specialty Johnson defines by particularity; and what is singular, cites for exemplification a passage from Hale, in which the word has its technical sense of a bond or instrument under seal. Yet this palpable error has escaped the observation of Mason, and been transcribed by other compilers into their dictionaries.

Boll is defined by Johnson "a round stalk or stem;" the verb to boll, "to rise in a stalk," "the flax was bolled." Ex. 9, 31. I have ever supposed the most unlettered reader of the bible to have a correct understanding of this passage; and the mistake of the lexicographer has always appeared to me a remarkable instance of negligence. Yet it may be accounted for. Boll, is the Saxon bolla, was the ancient correct orthography of bowl, and probably is derived from the Hebrew gebōl, the word used in this passage. The translators unqestionably used this old orthography of bowl, which Johnson mistook for bole, a stem, and without examining the original, explained it in conformity with that idea. But the real sense of the passage is, that the seed vessel of the flax, the pericarp or capsule, was formed. The Seventy translate the Hebrew by spermatizon, seeded, or seeding, and this sense is rendered certain by the corresponding term used to denote the state of the barley, abib, eared or being in the ear.

This error of Johnson, however obvious, has been transcribed by most or all later compilers of English dictionaries. It is received also into the Latin dictionaries of Ainsworth and Entick; into the Dutch dictionary of Willcocks, the German of Fahrenkruger, by N. Bailey; the French of Boyer and the Italian of Montucci.

This fact is a remarkable proof of the indolence of authors, of their confidence in the opinions of a great man, and their willingness to live upon the labors of others. It shows us also the extensive mischiefs resulting from the mistakes of an eminent author, and the danger of taking his opinions upon trust.

Johnson's mistake in the definition of clout is the more remarkable, as it proves him to have misinterpreted his favorite author, Shakespear, as well as Milton. The clouted brogues and clouted shoon of of those poets were shoes with soles studded with nails; such shoes as our country people have worn within my memory, and I am told, still wear, in some parts of America. Johnson supposed the word clouted to signify patched or mended coarsely—an error which the passage cited from Shakespear readily detects, for the "clouted brogues" were put off, to prevent the nails from making too much noise.

But the instances in which Johnson has wholly mistaken the sense of words, are far less numerous than those in which he has failed to explain the appropriate senses of words apparently synonymous. Thus abdicate and resign may, by negligent writers, be used in nearly the same sense. But in strictness, each has a distinct appropriate and technical sense—abdication denoting the abandonment of an office or trust without formality, and resignation, the voluntary surrender of a commission or office to the constituent.

Alleviate, says Johnson, is to "make light, to ease, to soften." True; but what is its appropriate sense? to what objects does it apply? a ship is made light by unloading, and a guinea is made light by clipping; but neither of them is alleviated. A metal is softened by fusion, tho it is not alleviated. The appropriate sense of the word is to make lighter or diminish an evil, or burden, as pain, grief, cares and the like; and a principal use of dictionaries is to mark this particular application of words.

To exemplify this word, Johnson cites from Harvey the following passage. "The pains taken in the speculative will much alleviate me in describing the practical part." Here alleviate is used for relieve; or the words my task ought to have been used insted of me. To alleviate me, is hardly English; and this is one of a multitude of instances, in which Johnson has cited as an authority what he should have condemned as an error.

Acquire, says Johnson, is "to gain by one's own labor, what is not received from nature, or transmitted by inheritance." Yet Blackstone writes with accuracy that "an heir acquires an estate by descent," B. 2. Ch. 14; And a plant acquires a green color from the solar rays, which is the work of nature and not of its own labor. Johnson has therefore wholly mistaken the appropriate sense of the word, deducing it from the manner of obtaining, rather than from the nature of the thing obtained. Acquire is to get or obtain something which becomes permanent or inherent in the possessor. We acquire titles to property, rights, qualities, andc. but the chemist who obtains spirit by distillation does not acquire it; nor do we acquire a book which we borrow.

This species of imperfection is one of the principal defects in all our dictionaries; it occurs in almost every page, defeating, in a great degree, the object of such works, and contributing to a want of precision which is a blemish in our best authors.

See Saxon Chronicle, by Gibson, page 149, 176, andc.

From the censure implied in this remark, I am not myself wholly free, having relied too much on certain modern authorities of eminent literary attainments. Since I have explored the more remote sources of our language, so many mistakes in our present systems of grammar have been detected, that I have declined to alienate the copy right of my own grammar, and shall not consent to a republication of it, until revised and amended.—The grammars of our language, now taught in our seminaries of learning, are rapidly banishing from books, some of its best established and most legitimate idioms.

ORTHOGRAPHY

The orthography of our language is extremely irregular; and many fruitless attempts have been made to reform it. The utility and expedience of such reform have been controverted, and both side of the question have been maintained with no inconsiderable zeal.

On this subject, as on most others which divide the opinions of men, parties seem to have erred by running into extremes. The friends of a reform maintain that our alphabet should be rendered perfectly regular, by rejecting superfluous characters, and introducing new ones to supply defects; so that every sound may be represented by a distinct letter, and no letter have more sounds than one. This scheme is impracticable, and not at all necessary.(1)

The opposers of a reform, on the other hand, contend that no alterations should be made in orthography, as they would not only occasion inconvenience, but tend to render old books useless, and obscure etymology. It is fortunate for the language and for those who use it, that this doctrin did not prevail in the reign of Henry the fourth; for it was as just then as it is now; and had all changes in spelling ceased at that period, what a spectacle of deformity would our language now exhibit! The doctrin is as mischievous in its consequences, as the reasons on which it is founded are false. Every man of common reading knows that a living language must necessarily suffer gradual changes in its current words, in the significations of many words, and in pronunciation. The unavoidable consequence then of fixing the orthography of a living language, is to destroy the the use of the alphabet. This effect has, in a degree, already taken place in our language; and letters, the most useful invention that ever blessed mankind, have lost and continue to lose a part of their value, by no longer being the representatives of the sounds originally annexed to them. Strange as it may seem the fact is undeniable, that the present doctrin that no change must be made in writing words, is destroying the benefits of an alphabet, and reducing our language to the barbarism of Chinese characters insted of letters. What is still stranger, this doctrin is pertinaciously maintained by the men who make pretenses to exquisit taste and refinement in polite literature. And if any thing can add to the contradictions which such a principle involves, it is that the same men, who object to the minutest alterations of orthography, are the most active in effecting changes of pronunciation; thus aiding to destroy the use of letters, by creating new differences between the written and spoken language.

The correct principle respecting changes in orthography seems to lie between these extremes of opinion. No great changes should ever be made at once, nor should any change be made which violates established principles, creates great inconvenience, or obliterates the radicals of the language. But gradual changes to accommodate the written to the spoken language, when they occasion none of these evils, and especially when they purify words from corruptions, improve the regular analogies of a language and illustrate etymology, are not only proper, but indispensable.

On this general principle have all learned and civilized nations proceeded in refining their languages and preserving the use of alphabetical writing. Hence we observe as great a difference between the orthography in the laws of Romulus, Servius Tullius and the Decemvirs, and that of Cicero and Livy, as between the orthography of Chaucer and that of Addison. This principle also prevailed universally in the English nation, from the revival of letters to the last century, when certain eminent authors adopted an idea, as absurd as incompatible with improvement, that a living language can be fixed beyond the possibility of change; and to the prevalence of this error, we may ascribe many of the irregularities of our present orthography.

From this error, or perhaps from a total inattention to the history of our language, has originated another mistake which now governs public opinion on this subject; this is, that the present state of our orthography exhibits the true etymology of words, and that every alteration would tend to obscure it. There are some classes of words of which this true; but let it be noted that no small part of the anomalies in the spelling of words, are egregious corruptions of the primitive orthography. Thus the present orthography of leather, feather, weather, stead, wealth, mould, son, ton, wonder, worship, thirst, andc. is corrupt; having been vitiated during the dark ages of English literature, under the Norman princes. The true orthography from the first Saxon writings to the 12th century, was lether, fether, wether, sted or stede, welga, mold, suna, tunna, wundor, wurthscipe, thurst.

Broad, was written brade, brede, and braed. We have preserved the first in the adjective broad, bu the pronunciation of the noun bredth we take from the second, and the orthograhy most absurdly from the last.(2)

Tongue, was in Saxon written tung, tonge or tunga, which we pronounce correctly tung, omitting the last letter as in other Saxon words, and yet we write the word most barbarously tongue. Launch from lance, is a corruption introduced at a very early period, with daunce for dance, auncient for ancient, maister for master, plaister for plaster, and numerous similar corruptions which mark the barbarism which succeeded the Norman conquest.

Heinous from the French haine, which is correctly pronounced hainous as it was formerly written, is such a palpable error that no lexicographer can be justified in giving it his sanction.

Though is also a vitious orthography; tho being much nearer to the original word.

Drought and height are corruptions of drugothe, heatho; which the Saxons formed from dryg and heh or heah, dry and high, by adding the termination th as in length from leng; strength from streng, and as we form truth from true, width from wide, warmth from warm. The Saxon termination th is universally preserved in the popular pronunciation of this country; and so far is it from being an error or corruption, that it is the very essence of the nouns, drouth and highth. Men therefore who use this pronunciation, tho chargeable with "a zeal for analogy," as Johnson observes of Milton, and tho they may not imitate Garrick as Walker does, will still have the honor to be correct, and to preserve the purity of the original orthography. They will further have the honor of conforming to what is in fact the national pronunciation, and has been, from the earliest records of our language. Height is an innovation comparatively modern; and drought is the Belgic dialect of the Teutonic; but neither of these words existed in the Saxon, the parent of our language.

The use of k at the end of words after c, deserves notice, as it affords a remarkable proof of the corruption of language by means of heedless writers. Johnson remarks that c, having no determinate sound, according to English orthography never ends a word. Had this eminent critic examined ancient authorities with more care, he would have found the reverse of his affirmation to be the truth. The practice, in his time, of closing all words with k after c, on which he founded his observation, was a Norman innovation.

The history of these letters is shortly this. The Romans used c as an equivalent for the Greek k, as appears by the translation of Greek into Latin, and of Latin into Greek, made while both were living languages. The Roman c is the Hebrew caph inverted and rounded at the angles, and the Greek kappa was probably formed from the same character. The Greek alphabet did not recognize c, nor the Roman alphabet k. When therefore the Romans borrowed and naturalized Greek words contining a k, they used for it their own equivalent letter c.

Hence the Greek keler, swift, was written in Latin cclcr; kentauros, a centaur, centaurus; keros, wax, cera; kio, to move, cieo; kinnabaris, cinnabar; kinnamon, cinnamum; mousikos, musicus; leaving not a particle of doubt that c and k were letters of precisely the same power.

The Saxons had probably no knowledge of letters, till they settled in England; and in that country, no letters were known, but those of the Roman alphabet, a knowledge of which had been left there by the Romans. The Saxons therefore adopted the Roman characters, with a few variations, which were required by particular sounds in their language. Hence, till after the conquest, c was used to express the power of k, as in the Latin language; and insted of not terminating any English word, as Johnson alleges, it terminated every word, where the power of k occured; as in boc, book; folc, folk; wic, wick; ric, rick. In a volume of Saxon history, written in the twelfth century, the letter k is not found in ten words.

The Norman conquest however effected a change in the power of c, and established it as the equivalent of s before e, i and y. This, like most innovations, introduced confusion, and rendered it convenient or necessary to use k in all words in which the power of k was wanted before those vowels. Thus the Saxon cepan, to keep; liccian, to lick; licean, to like; locian, to look, were converted into the present English words; and in many words, k usurped the place of c without a like necessity, as book from boc. Hence we find that in most of our Saxon words, k is written at the end, after c or in lieu of it; and we cannot, without it, form the past time and participle of verbs; for liced, loced would lead to a false pronunciation.

Such is the history of the introduction of k into our language. But c at the end of words retains its place and power, particularly in all words formed from Greek and Latin adjectives in kos and cus, and consequently in all words not from the same originals, but formed according to that analogy; as music, public, republic, nitric, camphoric, majestic. To add k after c in such words is beyond measure absurd, for both have the same power, having been formed from the same original character. If any thing can add to the impropriety, it is that k is always omitted in the derivatives, musical, publication, republican. Uniformity is a prime excellence in the rules of language, and surely no person will contend for the propriety of musickal, publickation and republickan. Fortunately, most modern writers have rejected the k from words in which it is useless; and it is desirable that dictionaries should add their authority to the practice.

We have a few words of another class which remain as outlaws in orthography. These are such as end in re, as sceptre, theatre, metre, mitre, nitre, lustre, sepulchre, spectre, and a few others. Most of these have found their way into our language from the Greek and Roman, through the channel of the French. This termination is common in the Saxon as well as the French, and probably the final e was pronounced after the consonant.

However this may have been, English writers have unanimously formed a different analogy by transposing the letters, so that the re in sceptre can not be considered as an English termination. And it is among the inconsistences which meet our observation in every part of orthography, that the French nombre, chambre, disastre, disordre, diametre, tigre, chartre, arbitre, tendre, fievre, entre, monstre, and the Saxon hongre, and hundreds of other words should be converted into number, chamber, disaster, disorder, andc. conformable to the pronunciation, and that lustre, sceptre, metre, and a few others hould be permitted to wear their foreign livery. This is the more surprising, as the most distinguished writers of the last and preceding centuries, Newton, Shaftibury, Dryden, Prideaux, Hook, Whiston, Bolingbroke, Middleton, andc. wrote these words in the regular English manner.

"Having the imperial scepter."—Newton chron. 308.

"The scepter of Babylon was broken."—Prideaux con. 1, 2.

See Boling, let. 8. Hook. Rom. hist. 1. 79. Whiston, Josephus, 2. 14. Hist. of California, 1. 71, andc. And this orthography gives sceptered, as written by Milton, Pope and other poets, which cannot be regularly formed from the French sceptre.

"The power of earth, and scepter'd sons of jove."—Pope Iliad, B. 1.

The present practice is not only contrary to the general uniformity observable in words of this class, but is inconsistent with itself; for Peter, a proper name, is always written in the English manner. Metre also retains its French spelling, while the same word in composition, as in diameter, barometer, and thermometer, is conformed to the English orthography. Such palpable inconsistencies and preposterous anomalies do no honor to English literature, but very much perplex the student, and offend the man of taste.

A like inconsistency is observable in another class of words which we receive from the French language. Musquet, masque, risque, paquet, picquet, chequer, relique, andc. have received a regular English orthography—musket, mask, risk, packet, picket, checker, relic, andc. while burlesque, grotesque, picturesque, pique and oblique retain their French livery. Opaque is now written opake, by most authors; and it is presumed that the few outlaws which remain, will soon be subjected to the laws of English orthography.

A similar inconsistency prevails in the pronunciation of the words of Greek original, beginning with arch, in which ch, receive their English sound before a consonant, as in archbishop, and the sound of k before a vowel, as in a architect. But arch, being established in its English pronunciation, becomes the root from which every word of this class is considered as derived, and will naturally control the pronunciation of the whole. Nor ought this principle of uniformity to be violated; for uniformity in the classes of words is the most convenient principle in the structure of language, and whatever arbitrary rules the learned may frame, the greatest part of men will be governed by habits of uniformity. To these habits we are indebted for all the regularity which is found in our own language or in any other.

For this reason, rather than from a rigid adherence to the originals, we ought to write defense, pretense, offense, recompense, andc. with s insted of c; for we always use that letter in the derivatives, defensive, offensive, pretension, recompensing.

For a like reason, as well as to purify our orthography from corruptions and restore to words their genuine spelling, we ought to reject u from honor, favor, candor, error, and others of this class. Under the Norman princes, when every effort of royal authority was exerted to crush the Saxons and obliterate their language, the Norman French was the only language of the English courts and legal proceedings, and the Latin words which, at that period, were introduced into use in England, came clothed with the French livery. At the same time, to preserve a trace of their originals, the o of the Latin honor, as well as the u of the French honeur was retained in the terminating syllable. Hence for some centuries, our language was disfigured with a class of mongrels, splendour, inferiour, superiour, authour, and the like, which are neither Latin nor French, nor calculated to exhibit the English pronunciation. Johnson, in reverence to usage, retained this vitious orthography, without regarding the palpable absurdity of inserting u in primitive words, when it must be omitted in the derivatives, supcriority, inferiority and the like; for no person ever wrote superiourity, inferiourity. A sense of propriety however, has nearly triumphed over these errors; and our best writers have almost unanimously rejected the u from this whole class of words, except perhaps ten or twelve. From these also Ash has very consistently rejected u, restoring the purity of the original orthography.

Johnson often committed errors, but seldom gave his sanction to innovations, unauthorized by any good principle. Yet in a few instances he has departed from his usual caution. An instance occurs in his change of sceptic to skeptic. This innovation had some countenance in the pronunciation which had been corrupted by the Universities; for Greek scholars had discovered that the original was skeptikos, from skeptomai. The mischiefs which proceed from such partial views of subjects are incalculable. It is a thing of no consequence whether we pronounce vowels and consonants as the Greeks and Romans pronounced them—but it is of immense practical importance, that when we have analogies established in our own language, we should, on no account, violate them by introducing unnecessary exceptions.

By immemorial usage, the English nation had established the Latin orthography of words of this class, as scene, from skene; scepter, from skeptron; sciamachy, from skiamachia; in which, contrary to the original sounds of the k and the c, sc had been pronounced as s. To change one word of this class, without the others, was to innovate without reason, or the prospect of utility; to deform our orthography with anomaly and embarrass the student with needless difficulties. The same reason would authorize skience for science; skiolist from sciolus, and skintillation from scintillatio; nay, civil must be written and pronounced kivil; celebrate, kelebrate, and circle, kircle; for in all words, c in Latin had the sound of k. Such are the mischiefs of innovation! Fortunately, the corrupt pronunciation of sceptic, has made little progress in this country; and in this, as in many other words, if we can be permitted to think and reason for ourselves, we may still preserve the purity of our language.

We have some classes of words received from the Latin through the French, to which a final e was anciently affixed, either for the purpose of forming a syllable or to soften a preceding vowel, in conformity with the established pronunciation of the French. Such are determine, examine, doctrine, discipline, medicine, and others with a different terminating syllable. This practice of ending words with e was doubtless warranted by the pronunciation, during the ages which followed the Norman conquest in England. In many cases of Saxon words ending in a, which formed a distinct syllable. I find the Normans changed the a into e, and the slight evanescent sound of this vowel being finally omitted in pronunciation, the vowel was at last retrenched. In other words, the French influence introduced a final e, in words of Saxon original, to which the Saxons affixed no vowel. But whatever reasons might once exist for the use of final e in poete, lande, behinde, businesse, and a multitude of other words, none surely can be assigned for annexing it to the words before mentioned. The letter does not belong to the originals, determino, examino, doctrina, andc. it has no use in modifying the preceding vowel; and it is never used in the derivative words, determination, examination, doctrinal, disciplinarian, medicinal; while in some classes of words, it leads to a false pronunciation. It is a relic of barbarism which ought not to be tolerated in the language. It ought to be retrenched, as it has been from origin and deposit.

In some words we observe most singular corruptions. Doubt, is the French doute, with a b inserted out of complasance to its Latin original dubito. Debt and indebted stand nearly on the same footing.

Redoubt, is the French redoute, corrupted perhaps by a supposed alliance of the word with doubt, with which it has not the least connection.

Pincers holds a place in books, tho rarely heard in pronunciation. This word is a remarkable proof of the inveteracy of custom, even when obviously wrong; for tho the verb pinch is formed immediately from the French pincer, yet the noun used in conversation is pinchers, the correct and regular derivative of the English verb, pinch.

The introduction of e into vineyard is a modern corruption; the word not being compounded of vine and yard, but of the primitive vin and yard, the correct pronunciation of which we retain. It is precisely analogous to wisdom, which is compounded of the ancient wis and dom. We might just as well write wisedom as vineyard. In this as in almost every other instance of anomaly, the pronunciation has been preserved correct by custom, while the orthography has been corrupted by authors.

It is singularly unfortunate, that English translators of foreign languages, have not uniformly translated letters as well as words. The practice of receiving foreign words into our language, in a foreign orthography, is one of the most serious and growing evils which the friends of an elegant and regular language have to combat. The powers of many of the letters are very different in different languages. When therefore a French, or a German word is introduced into English, the letters should be translated—and the true sounds of the foreign words expressed in English characters of correspondent powers. Thus soup in French, when the letters are translated, becomes soop in English—tour becomes toor—schistus in German, is shistus in English—pacha, bedouin, in French are pasha, or bashaw and bedoween in English—Wolga in German is Volga in English; Michigan, Chenango in French are Mishigan, Shenango in English. The great body of a nation cannot possibly know the powers of letters in a foreign language; and the practice of introducing foreign words in a foreign orthography, generates numerous diversities of pronunciation, and perplexes the mass of a nation. And the practice is, I believe, peculiar to the English. The Romans gave to all foreign words, their own letters, terminations and inflections; and a similar practice obtains among the modern nations on the Continent of Europe.

There are other corruptions of English orthography, which may be mentioned; but these examples are sufficient to show, first, the extreme negligence of authors, whose business it is to purify and refine orthography, no less than to enrich the language with new terms and improve its general structure. Secondly, the utter mistake entertained by superficial observers, in supposing our present orthography to be correctly deduced from the originals.

A few of these errors may still be corrected, as the emendations will require trifling changes, which can occasion no perceptible inconvenience; while they will purify the orthography, illustrate etymology and relieve the learner from embarrassment.

But it would be useless to attempt any change, even if practicable, in those anomalies which form whole classes of words, and in which, change would rather perplex than ease the learner. That h is pronounced before w in when, tho written after it; and that tion are pronounced shon or shun, are things of no great inconvenience; for these irregularities, occurring uniformly in many words, which constitute classes, form the anomalies into general rules, which are as easily learnt as any other general principles.

(1) In the year 1786, Dr. Franklin proposed to me to prosecute his scheme of a Reformed Alphabet, and offered me his types for the purpose. I declined accepting his offer, on a full conviction of the utter impracticability, as well as inutility of the scheme. The orthography of our language might be rendered sufficiently regular, without a single new character, by means of a few trifling alterations of the present characters, and retrenching a few superfluous letters, the most of which are corruptions of the original words.

(2) Chaucer wrote brede; and bredth the true orthography is preserved in the first Charter of Massachusetts, Haz, Col. Vol. 1, p, 240, 241, 213, as it is in many old authors.

PRONUNCIATION

The pronunciation of words is a subject which presents even greater difficulties than the orthography; and difficulties which multiply in proportion to the efforts made to surmount them. The friends of refinement have entertained sanguine expectations, that men of letters might agree upon some standard by which pronunciation might be regulated, and reduced to a good degree of uniformity. My own hopes of such an event are very much abated by the ill success of the ingenious compilers of standards in Great Britain; and the more I reflect upon the subject, the more I am convinced that a living language admits of no fixed state, nor of any certain standard of pronunciation by which even the learned in general will consent to be governed. Elphinstone adopted the visionary idea of a perfect alphabet and fell into disrepute. Kenrick did not reach the point of refinement demanded by the Court and Stage, and was neglected. Sheridan carried his refinement and his fashionable peculiarities so far, that the nation almost unanimously rejected a great part of his scheme. Walker succeeded, condemned one half of Sheridan's court pronunciation, and for a short period, enjoyed a tide of popularity. Nares, whose work I have not seen but whose reputation stands high even with Walker and his other competitors, condemns Walker in some particulars; and Jones, the latest compiler of distinction and popularity, sweeps a large part of Walker's peculiarities of pronunciation, into the lumber-room of corruptions. Who is to succeed and condemn them all, is yet uncertain; but it is not to be doubted that the next period of twenty years will produce as many standard authors, as the last, no two of which will agree in their scheme of pronunciation.

That a complete standard, to which all the polite and learned of a nation will conform, is, in its own nature, impracticable, may be satisfactorily proved from the structure of the human mind; from the various modes in which different men view the same subject; the different effect of the same degrees of evidence on different minds; the different impressions made by education, which become the ground-work of uncontrollable prejudices; and the extreme reluctance which men feel in relinquishing their peculiar notions, and yielding to the opinions of others. The same consequence may be deduced from the variableness of pronunciation among the leading characters of a nation. So far is the present pronunciation of the court and stage in England from being fixed, that no two writers are yet agreed what it is; and if the case were otherwise, there is no probability that it would remain the same for any considerable time. Any man who will read Sheridan, Walker and Jones, will be satisfied not only that there is no uniformity in what is called the best pronunciation, but that such attempts as have hitherto been made to ascertain and establish a standard, render it impossible there ever should be one; and that every succeeding compiler only multiplies the obstacles to the accomplishment of his own wishes. Every compiler has some peculiarities in his scheme; some local practices to which he is accustomed, and which he mistakes for the best pronunciaton. Both Sheridan and Walker abound with such local usages. The more books are made, the more local usages will be exalted into a standard of correctness, each of which will have adherents, and the more the honest inquirer will be perplexed and confounded with various usages and discordant principles.

To satisfy my readers that I do not exagerate the difficulties of this subject and the contradictions between the most respectable standard authors, I will here exhibit a few examples, in which the pronunciation of each author is given, not in his own letters and figures, for these might not be understood by persons unacquainted with his works; but in letters of known powers, and which the most ordinary reader cannot mistake.

SHERIDAN.

WALKER.

JONES.

Ab'bey, abby

Ab'bee

Ab'by

Abbrévyate

Abbréveeate

Abbrévyate.

Abbrévyature

Abbréveeachure

Abbrévyature

Ab'dicate

Ab'deecate

Ab'dicate

Abdic'ativ

Ab'dicativ

Ab'dicativ

Abdom'inak

Abdom'eenal

Abdom'inal

Aberun'cate

Abeeruncate

Aberun'cate

Abee'ance

Abáyance

Abáyance

Ab'jectly

Ab'jectlee

Ab'jectly

Abil'ity

Abil'eetee

Abil'ity

Ab'lepsy

Ab'lepsee

Ab'lepsy

Ab'negate

Ab'neegate

Abnegate

Abominátion

Abomeenátion

Abomination

Abor'tively.

Abor'tivelee

Abortively

Abrupt'ly

Abrupt'lee

Abruptly

Abscis'sion

Abcizhon

Abscizhon

Absin'thyated

Absintheeated

Absinthyated

Abstémyus

Abstémeeus

Abstéemyus

Abstémyusly

Abstémeeusly

Absteémyusly

Abstémyusness

Abstémeeusness

Absteémyusness

Ab'stinence

Ab'steenence.

Ab'stinence

Ab'stinent

Ab'steenent

Ab'stinent

Abstract'edly.

Abstract'edlee

Abstract'edly

It will be observed that the principal difference in the foregoing table, is in the sound of i and y, in unaccented syllables; Walker directing the sound to be uttered as the long e in me, see. Thus according to his scheme, ability, vanity are to be pronounced abileetee, vaneetee; which, as Jones has justly observed, is no "trivial error." Indeed this error is so material, as to render his book a very improper guide to pronunciation. It is utterly repugnant to the genius of our language—and if followed, would totally destroy the harmony of our metrical composition. Let these lines be read with Walker's pronunciation.
"The proper studee of mankind is man"—
"A being darklee wise and rudelee great"—
We see at once the pernicious effects of this scheme of pronunciation, in the confusion of poetic feet and loss of melody.1
This mistake of Walker's, extends to a greater number of words, than any other—It extends literally to thousands. Sheridan and Jones have abioded it, and given to the i and y unaccented, the short sound of e, which corresponds with the practice in the United States.
Let the differences of pronunciation be noted also in the following words.

SHERIDAN.

WALKER.

JONES.

Bench, andc.

Bentsh

Bensh

Bentsh

Beltsh

Belsh

Beltsh

Filtsh

Filsh

Filtsh

Brantsh

Bransh

Brantsh

Intsh

Insh

Intsh

Pintsh

Pinsh

Pintsh

Buntsh

Bunsh

Buntsh

In this class of words, Sheridan and Jones are unquestionably right; and with them corresponds the practice of this country. Where Walker learnt to give the French sound of ch, to such words, I cannot conceive.

SHERIDAN.

WALKER.

JONES.

Accentuation.

Accenchuation

Accentuation.

Gratulation

Grachulation

Gratulation

Habitual

Habichual

Habitual

Furnichur

Furneeture

Furniture

Multichood

Multeetude

Multitude

Protrood

Protrude

Protrude

Prochooberant

Protuberant

Protuberant

Shooperb

Superb

Superb

Chooter

Tutor

Tutor

Choomult

Tumult

Tumult

These examples are selected from whole classes of words, consisting of many hundreds, in which each author has prescribed to himself some rule which he deems so clearly correct, as to admit of no doubt or controversy. And how is the honest inquirer to know which is right, or whether either of them is entitled to be a standard authority? Do not such pointed differences, among authors of distinction, prove that there is no uniformity of pronunciation among the higher ranks of society in Great Britain; and consequently, that no standard can be found in their practice? This unquestionably is a fair inference from the facts.

1 Palpable as this error is, we find Murray has introduced it, with other mistakes of Walker, into his Spelling Book; giving a whole table of such words as daily, safely, holy, nobly, andc. with directions to pronounce "both the syllables long."

Made in the USA
Middletown, DE
31 March 2023